TOUGH
QUESTIONS
REVISED EDITION

DON'T ALL RELIGIONS LEAD TO GOD?

The Tough Questions Series

DON'T ALL

RELIGIONS

LEAD TO

GOD?

DON'T ALL RELIGIONS LEAD TO GOD?

GARRY POOLE

foreword by **Lee Strobel**

**WILLOW
CREEK**
RESOURCES

ZONDERVAN™

GRAND RAPIDS, MICHIGAN 49530 USA

We want to hear from you. Please send your comments about this book to us in care of zreview@zondervan.com. Thank you.

ZONDERVAN™

Don't All Religions Lead to God?
Copyright © 1998, 2003 by Willow Creek Association

Requests for information should be addressed to:

Zondervan, *Grand Rapids, Michigan 49530*

ISBN: 0-310-24506-0

Interior design by Nancy Wilson

Printed in the United States of America

06 07 08 09 /❖ CH/ 10 9 8 7 6

Contents

Foreword

For most of my life I was an atheist. I thought that the Bible was hopelessly riddled with mythology, that God was a man-made creation born of wishful thinking, and that the deity of Jesus was merely a product of legendary development. My no-nonsense education in journalism and law contributed to my skeptical viewpoint. In fact, just the idea of an all-powerful, all-loving, all-knowing creator of the universe seemed too absurd to even justify the time to investigate whether there could be any evidence backing it up.

However, my agnostic wife's conversion to Christianity, and the subsequent transformation of her character and values, prompted me to launch my own spiritual journey in 1980. Using the skills I developed as the legal affairs editor of *The Chicago Tribune,* I began to check out whether any concrete facts, historical data, or convincing logic supported the Christian faith. Looking back, I wish I had this curriculum to supplement my efforts.

This excellent material can help you in two ways. If you're already a Christ-follower, this series can provide answers to some of the tough questions your seeker friends are asking—or you're asking yourself. If you're not yet following Christ but consider yourself either an open-minded skeptic or a spiritual seeker, this series can also help you in your journey. You can thoroughly and responsibly explore the relevant issues while discussing the topics in community with others. In short, it's a tremendous guide for people who really want to discover the truth about God and this fascinating and challenging Nazarene carpenter named Jesus.

If the previous paragraph describes you in some way, prepare for the adventure of a lifetime. Let the pages that follow take you on a stimulating journey of discovery as you grapple with the most profound—and potentially life-changing—questions in the world.

—Lee Strobel, author of
The Case for Christ and *The Case for Faith*

Getting Started

Welcome to the Tough Questions series! This small group curriculum was produced with the conviction that claims regarding spiritual truth can and should be tested. Religions—sometimes considered exempt from scrutiny—are not free to make sweeping declarations and demands without providing solid reasons why they should be taken seriously. These teachings, including those from the Bible in particular, purport to explain the most significant of life's mysteries, with consequences alleged to be eternal. Such grand claims should be analyzed carefully. If this questioning process exposes faulty assertions, it only makes sense to refuse to place one's trust in these flawed systems of belief. If, on the other hand, an intense investigation leads to the discovery of truth, the search will have been worth it all.

Christianity contends that God welcomes sincere examination and inquiry; in fact, it's a matter of historical record that Jesus encouraged such scrutiny. The Bible is not a secret kept only for the initiated few, but an open book available for study and debate. The central teachings of Christianity are freely offered to all, to the skeptic as well as to the believer.

So here's an open invitation: explore the options, examine the claims, and draw your conclusions. And once you encounter and embrace the truth—look out! Meaningful life-change and growth will be yours to enjoy.

It is possible for any of us to believe error; it is also feasible for us to resist truth. Using this set of discussion guides will help you sort out the true from the supposed, and ultimately offer a reasonable defense of the Christian faith. Whether you are a nonbeliever or

> You will seek me and find me when you seek me with all your heart.
> —Jeremiah 29:13

skeptic, or someone who is already convinced and looking to fortify your faith, these guides will lead you to a fascinating exploration of vital spiritual truths.

Tough Questions for Small Groups

The Tough Questions series is specifically designed to give spiritual seekers (or non-Christians) a chance to raise questions and investigate the basics of the Christian faith within the safe context of a seeker small group. These groups typically consist of a community of two to twelve seekers and one or two leaders who gather on a regular basis, primarily to discuss spiritual matters. Seeker groups meet at a wide variety of locations, from homes and offices to restaurants and churches to bookstores and park district picnic tables. A trained Christian leader normally organizes the group and facilitates the discussions based on the seekers' spiritual concerns and interests. Usually, at least one apprentice (or coleader) who is also a Christian assists the group leader. The rest of the participants are mostly, if not all, non-Christians. This curriculum is intended to enhance these seeker small group discussions and create a fresh approach to exploring the Christian faith.

Because the primary audience is the not-yet-convinced seeker, these guides are designed to represent the skeptical, along with the Christian, perspective. While the truths of the Christian position are strongly affirmed, it is anticipated that non-Christians will dive into these materials with a group of friends and discover that their questions and doubts are not only well understood and represented here, but also valued. If that goal is accomplished, open and honest discussions about Christianity can follow. The greatest hope behind the formation of this series is that seekers will be challenged in a respectful way to seriously consider and even accept the claims of Christ.

A secondary purpose behind the design of this series is to provide a tool for small groups of Christians to use as they discuss answers to the tough questions seekers are asking. The process of wrestling through these important questions and issues will not only strengthen their own personal faith, but also provide them with insights for entering into informed dialogues about Christianity with their seeking friends.

A hybrid of the two options mentioned above may make more sense for some groups. For example, a small group of Christians may want to open up their discussion to include those who are just beginning to investigate spiritual things. This third approach provides an excellent opportunity for both Christians and seekers to examine the claims of Christianity together. Whatever the configuration of your group, may you benefit greatly as you use these guides to fully engage in lively discussions about issues that matter most.

Guide Features

The Introduction

At the beginning of every session is an introduction, usually several paragraphs long. You may want to read this beforehand even though your leader will probably ask the group to read it aloud together at the start of every meeting. These introductions are written from a skeptical point of view, so a full spectrum of perspectives is represented in each session. Hopefully, this information will help you feel represented, understood, and valued.

Open for Discussion

Most sessions contain ten to fifteen questions your group can discuss. You may find that it is difficult for your group to get through all these questions in one sitting. That is okay; the important thing is to engage in the topic at hand—not to necessarily get through every question. Your group, however, may decide to spend more than one meeting on each session in order to address all of the questions. The Open for Discussion questions in these sessions are designed to draw out group participation and give everyone the opportunity to process things openly.

Usually, the first question of each session is an "icebreaker." These simple questions are designed to get the conversation going by prompting the group to discuss a nonthreatening issue, usually having to do with the session topic to be covered. Your group may want to make time for additional icebreakers at the beginning of each discussion.

Heart of the Matter

The section called "Heart of the Matter" represents a slight turn in the group discussion. Generally speaking, the questions in this section speak more to the emotional, rather than just the intellectual, side of the issue. This is an opportunity to get in touch with how you feel about a certain aspect of the topic being discussed and to share those feelings with the rest of the group.

Charting Your Journey

The purpose of the "Charting Your Journey" section is to challenge you to go beyond a mere intellectual and emotional discussion to personal application. This group experience is, after all, a journey, so each session includes this section devoted to helping you identify and talk about your current position. Your views will most likely fluctuate as you make new discoveries along the way.

Straight Talk

Every session has at least one section, called "Straight Talk," designed to stimulate further thinking and discussion around relevant supplementary information. The question immediately following Straight Talk usually refers to the material just presented, so it is important that you read and understand this part before you attempt to answer the question.

Quotes

Scattered throughout every session are various quotes, many of them from skeptical or critical points of view. These are simply intended to spark your thinking about the issue at hand.

Scripture for Further Study

This section ends each session with a list of suggested Scripture passages that relate to the discussion topic.

Recommended Resources

This section at the back of each guide lists recommended books that may serve as helpful resources for further study.

Discussion Guidelines

These guides, which consist mainly of questions to be answered in your group setting, are designed to elicit dialogue rather than short, simple answers. Strictly speaking, these guides are not Bible studies, though they regularly refer to biblical themes and passages. Instead, they are topical discussion guides, meant to get you talking about what you really think and feel. The sessions have a point and attempt to lead to some resolution, but they fall short of providing the last word on any of the questions raised. That is left for you to discover for yourself! You will be invited to bring your experience, perspective, and uncertainties to the discussion, and you will also be encouraged to compare your beliefs with what the Bible teaches in order to determine where you stand as each meeting unfolds.

Your group should have a discussion leader. This facilitator can get needed background material for each session in the *Tough Questions Leader's Guide*. There, your leader will find some brief points of clarification and understanding (along with suggested answers) for many of the questions in each session. The supplemental book *Seeker Small Groups* is also strongly recommended as a helpful resource for leaders to effectively start up small groups and facilitate discussions for spiritual seekers. *The Complete Book of Questions: 1001 Conversation Starters for Any Occasion,* a resource filled with icebreaker questions, may be a useful tool to assist everyone in your group to get to know one another better, and to more easily launch your interactions.

In addition, keep the following list of suggestions in mind as you prepare to participate in your group discussions.

1. The Tough Questions series does not necessarily need to be discussed sequentially. These guides as well as individual sessions can be mixed and matched in any order and easily discussed independently of each other, based on everyone's interests and questions.

2. If possible, read over the material before each meeting. Familiarity with the topic will greatly enrich the time you spend in the group discussion.

3. Be willing to join in the group interaction. The leader of the group will not present a lecture but rather will encourage each of you to openly discuss your opinions and disagreements. Plan to share your ideas honestly and forthrightly.

4. Be sensitive to the other members of your group. Listen attentively when they speak and be affirming whenever you can. This will encourage

more hesitant members of the group to participate. Always remember to show respect toward the others even if they don't always agree with your position.

5. Be careful not to dominate the discussion. By all means participate, but allow others to have equal time.

6. Try to stick to the topic being studied. There won't be enough time to handle the peripheral tough questions that come to mind during your meeting.

7. It would be helpful for you to have a good modern translation of the Bible, such as the New International Version, the New Living Translation, or the New American Standard Bible. You might prefer to use a Bible that includes notes especially for seekers, such as *The Journey: The Study Bible for Spiritual Seekers*. Unless noted otherwise, questions in this series are based on the New International Version.

8. Do some extra reading in the Bible and other recommended books as you work through these sessions. To get you started, the "Scripture for Further Study" section lists several Bible references related to each discussion, and the "Recommended Resources" section at the back of each guide offers some ideas of books to read.

Unspeakable Love

Christianity stands or falls on Christ. Yet he left us with a whole lot of hard sayings. But the central scandal of Christianity is that at a point in history, God came down to live among us in a person, Jesus of Nazareth. And the most baffling moment of Jesus' life was on the cross, where he hung to die like a common criminal. In that place of weakness—where all seemed lost, where the taunts of "Prove yourself, Jesus, and come down from there!" lashed out like the whip that flogged him prior to his crucifixion—somehow God was at his best. There at the cross, he expressed a love greater than words could ever describe. That act of Jesus, presented as the ultimate demonstration of the love and justice of God, begs to be put to "cross" examination.

As you wrestle with these tough questions, be assured that satisfying, reasonable answers are waiting to be found. And you're invited to discover them with others in your small group as you explore and discuss these guides. God bless you on your spiritual journey!

Seek and you will find; knock and the door will be opened to you.

—Matthew 7:7

Don't All Religions Lead to God?

There are over 1.3 billion Muslims in the world today, 900 million Hindus, 360 million Buddhists, 14 million Jews, and 1.9 billion Christians. That means, including those of no religious affiliation, there are nearly four billion people alive today who are not followers of Jesus Christ. According to the teachings of Christianity, not one of these people has "a prayer" (spiritually speaking). They will never experience God's endless grace. Without Jesus, these folks are without salvation—lost forever.

Are Christians really so narrow-minded and bigoted as to think these people will be excluded from heaven just because they happened to follow the wrong religion or were raised in the wrong culture? We all know family members, close friends, neighbors, and business associates who are good, moral people even though they embrace a different religion or no faith at all. Will these people really face eternal judgment?

John Hick, a strong critic of such exclusivity, writes angrily, "The extreme [Christian] who believes that all Muslims go to hell is probably not so much ignorant . . . as blinded by dark dogmatic spectacles through which he can see no good in religious devotion outside his own."

It's hard to imagine what compels Christians to limit the road to God and make it so narrow. Especially when the God they talk about is supposed to love and care about all people. Why wouldn't he throw open the doors of heaven and let everyone enter? Why spurn the prayers of a devout Muslim, for example, yet accept the prayers of a casual Christian— just because he or she belongs to the "right" spiritual group?

In this study, we'll take a look at what other world religions teach and compare each with Christianity. We'll also look at two prominent groups that claim to be Christian (Jehovah's Witnesses and Mormons) to see how their doctrines compare with biblical Christian teaching. Then you'll have the chance to wrestle with the implications of a message that says all these outside groups are missing the crucial ingredient.

Has God opened many roads to himself? Does he put barriers in the way of sincere seekers who are members of non-Christian religions? Is the narrow-minded view of a few Christians really the only way to know God now and live with him forever? Fasten your seat belts and get ready for some fast-paced discussion around these tough questions!

Don't All Religions Teach Basically the Same Thing?

What's the Big Deal Anyway?

The audience was in an uproar. Tempers were flaring. Shouts came from every corner in the room. The panel of experts seated in a row onstage tried to answer the questions being hurled at them like hand grenades. The talk show host ran from aisle to aisle, shoving the microphone at open mouths. Some waited for amplification; most didn't. The show's producer nudged the controller in the booth and grinned. "Nothin' like talkin' about religion to bring out the best—and worst—in people!"

It was sweeps week. And it was beautiful.

"What's the big deal anyway?" one woman from the back row shouted. "At least I believe in something. That's more than some people I know!"

"Come on, lady." A burly man front and center snatched the microphone and turned to her. "Do you really think everyone is right?" He shook his head and tightened his grip on the microphone as the host struggled to retrieve it. "How can opposite beliefs both be true? It's impossible."

An expert tried to speak up.

He didn't succeed.

"Buddha, Allah, Jesus," started a blonde in the middle section, "they're all the same. What does this 'higher power'"—she made quotation marks with her fingers—"care what we call him?"

"Or her," shouted an emotionally charged panelist from onstage.

"Right!" the blonde said. "Or her. What does 'it'"—again with the hand-enhanced quotation marks—"care what name we use?"

Those who agreed clapped and cheered as the show went to a commercial; those who didn't pulled the pins on their verbal grenades and laid in wait for the next round.

What does God care about the way we designate him or the way we choose to worship him? And why get so uptight about it? Doesn't life have enough trouble without us arguing over whose God is the "right" God and what hat you should wear to church on Sunday— or Saturday or the second Wednesday or whatever the case may be? In her book *Bird by Bird,* Anne Lamott said, "Now, if you ask me, what's going on is that we're all up to HERE in it, and probably the most important thing is that we not yell at one another." She has a point—it's not God who seems picky, it's people. Why would God care about such trivial matters as who has just the right perspective or the precise theological terminology? There are as many opinions as there are people. Surely there is more than one path to God.

Or is there?

OPEN FOR DISCUSSION

1. Why do you think there are so many religions in the world?

2. Do you think all the major religions are fundamentally the same or fundamentally different? If you can, give reasons to back up your answer.

3. True or false: If a religion inspires people to live better lives, we shouldn't question it. Explain your reasoning.

4. What difference, if any, would it make if the source of an idea or concept of great value to you was false?

5. True or false: People who claim to have the only truth about religion are arrogant, and such conceited attitudes are the cause of great strife and conflict in the world. Give an explanation for your answer.

STRAIGHT TALK

An Indian Legend: Six Blind Men and the Elephant

It was six men of Indostan
To learning much inclined,
Who went to see the Elephant
(Though all of them were blind),
That each by observation
Might satisfy his mind.
The First approached the Elephant,
And happening to fall
Against his broad and sturdy side,
At once began to bawl:
"God bless me! but the Elephant
Is very like a wall!"
The Second, feeling of the tusk,
Cried, "Ho! what have we here,
So very round and smooth and sharp?
To me 'tis mighty clear
This wonder of an Elephant
Is very like a spear!"
The Third approached the animal,
And happening to take
The squirming trunk within his hands,
Thus boldly up he spake:
"I see," quoth he, "the Elephant

Is very like a snake!"
The Fourth reached out an eager hand,
And felt about the knee:
"What most this wondrous beast is like
Is mighty plain," quoth he;
"'Tis clear enough the Elephant
Is very like a tree!"
The Fifth, who chanced to touch the ear,
Said: "E'en the blindest man
Can tell what this resembles most;
Deny the fact who can,
This marvel of an Elephant
Is very like a fan!"
The Sixth no sooner had begun
About the beast to grope,
Than, seizing on the swinging tail
That fell within his scope.
"I see," quoth he, "the Elephant
Is very like a rope!"
And so these men of Indostan
Disputed loud and long,
Each in his own opinion
Exceeding stiff and strong,
Though each was partly in the right,
They all were in the wrong!

— John Godfrey Saxe (1816–87)

---

6. How does the above legend apply to the issue of searching for and finding the truth about God and religion? Do you agree with its conclusion? Why or why not?

To overlook obvious differences between religions might seem broad-minded. In reality it is about as proud and narrow as a person could get. To say all religions are basically the same is to claim to be smarter than each of the billions of people who believe the unique aspects of their religion are of supreme importance to God. It is to claim that even though you are not an expert in their religion, you know they are wrong—you know their religion is really no different.

—Grantley Morris

7. How likely does it seem to you that any one religion would have the final say on what is true or not? Explain.

8. Does it seem reasonable to expect all religions to be true in their own ways, in spite of significant differences? Why or why not?

Even though many religions seem to be the same on the surface, the closer one gets to the central teachings, the more apparent the differences become. It is totally incorrect to say that all religions are the same.

—Josh McDowell, *Answers to Tough Questions Skeptics Ask About the Christian Faith*

9. Explain the significant differences behind the following two motivations for belief.

- "Christianity is true because I think it so, and you should agree with me."
- "Christianity is true because Jesus thought it so, and I agree with him."

STRAIGHT TALK

Toleration or Validation?

Sometimes, as people attempt to accept widely diverse religious teachings, truth is sacrificed. R. C. Sproul confronts this issue:

> I once had a conversation with a Bahai priest. He told me that all religions were equally valid. I began to interrogate him concerning the points of conflict that exist between Islam and Buddhism, between Confucianism and Judaism, and between Christianity and Taoism. The man responded by saying that he didn't know anything about Islam, Judaism, or the rest but that he did know they were all the same. I wondered aloud how anyone could assert that all religions were the same when he had no knowledge of what those religions professed or denied. How can Buddhism be true when it denies the existence of a personal God and at the same time Christianity be true when it affirms the existence of a personal God? Can there be a personal God and not be a personal God at the same time? . . . Can orthodox Judaism be right when it denies life after death and Christianity be equally right when it affirms life after death? Can classical Islam have a valid ethic that endorses the killing of infidels while at the same time the Christian ethic of loving your enemies be equally valid?
>
> —R. C. Sproul, *Reason to Believe*

The need of the moment is not one religion, but mutual respect and tolerance of the different religions.

—Mohandas Gandhi

If issues of religion have eternal consequences, then errors in thinking are infinitely tragic. To rephrase Karl Marx, false religion is the opiate of the people. It soothes, but does not cure.

—Greg Koukl, *Clear Thinking*

10. What is the difference between *toleration* of all religions and *validation* of all religions?

11. Do you think that in order for one religion to be true, all other religions must be *completely* false? (Do you think the six men in the Indian legend were each *completely* wrong?) Explain.

HEART OF THE MATTER

12. Do Christianity's exclusive claims worry, bother, or embarrass you? How has your reaction changed over time? Explain.

STRAIGHT TALK

Too Exclusive?

Even among Christians, the claim that Jesus is the only way creates a problem. For instance, Peter Kreeft and Ronald Tacelli write,

> In teaching apologetics (the defense of faith) and philosophy of religion for many years, we have found that students worry more and are embarrassed by Christianity's "un-American" exclusivist claims than about any other aspect of their religion. In an age of toleration and pluralism, the most popular argument against the Christian religion seems to be simply that it is only one of many religions. The world is a big place, "Different strokes for different folks," "live and let live," "don't impose your values on others."
>
> — *Handbook of Christian Apologetics*

13. Is it confusing or frustrating to you that there are so many different religions from which to choose? Why or why not?

14. If religions are all different, why do you think God allows so many of them to exist? Why doesn't he just narrow down the choices so it's easier to find him?

CHARTING YOUR JOURNEY

With this session you're beginning a journey. Keep in mind that you do not need to feel pressured to "say the right thing" at any point during these discussions. You're taking the time to do this work because you're looking for answers and because you're willing to be honest about your doubts and uncertainties. Others in your group would also benefit from hearing about what you'll be learning. So use these sessions profitably—ask the tough questions, think "outside the box," and learn from what others in your group have to say. But stay authentic about where you are in your journey.

To help you identify your progress more clearly, throughout this guide you will have opportunities to indicate where you are in your spiritual journey. As you gain more spiritual insights, you may find yourself reconsidering your opinions from session to session.

The important thing is for you to be completely truthful about what you believe—or don't believe—right now.

15. On a scale from one to ten, place an *X* near the spot and phrase that best describes your position at this point. Share your selection with the rest of the group and give reasons for placing your *X* where you did.

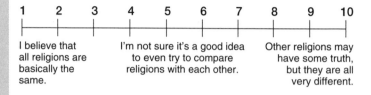

Scripture for Further Study

- Isaiah 53:6
- Proverbs 14:12
- Matthew 7:13–27
- Matthew 10:32–33
- Matthew 15:1–9
- Matthew 16:21–23
- Matthew 22:1–14
- Matthew 23:1–39
- Matthew 25:31–46
- Mark 9:7
- John 1:12, 14
- John 3:16

- John 14:6
- John 17:17b
- Acts 4:12
- Romans 3:23
- Romans 5:8, 12–21
- 1 Corinthians 1:18–19
- 1 Corinthians 3:10–17
- 1 Corinthians 15:3–4
- 2 Corinthians 5:1–10
- Ephesians 2:8–9
- 1 John 5:20

Isn't It Enough to Be Sincere?

Do Your Best

A mom looks at her child's drawing, created during kindergarten class. What a splendid work of art! She puts it on the refrigerator with glowing praise for the budding artist's talent. When Dad gets home, he admires his gifted little girl's efforts and showers her with accolades.

Of course, neither parent thinks the drawing should be displayed in a museum. But the truth is, they couldn't be more delighted in what their child has produced, and they mean it when they heap praise on her. Both the parents and the child have sincerely offered their love, and the work of art is valued for what it is.

Isn't that a picture of how God treats us? He knows we're trying and he knows our lives aren't perfect. Because he loves us, he accepts whatever we offer, without getting bogged down in harsh criticism. Surely, if he's the loving heavenly Father whom Jesus talked about, he can't be worried about a perfection we can't deliver. As long as we're trying, isn't that enough? What kind of tyrant would he be if he demanded more? Would we even want to spend eternity with such a God?

There are some, of course, who think God is keeping score. If we come up just a little short, he'll exclude us. These people describe a God who is apparently very put off when people pronounce his name wrong or don't follow every one of his rules perfectly. Such people are those who dot every *i* and cross every *t*, and they project the same concern with nitpicky details upon God. They live trying to figure out God and how to get life perfect, while the rest of us trust that a God of love is forgiving and willing to allow for our mistakes.

What kind of God do you believe in? How are you living your life—fearful at every turn that you might be one step out of line, or confident that in the end your sincere efforts will be enough? Your view of God will not only drastically alter your confidence level, it will impact how you live.

OPEN FOR DISCUSSION

1. Think of a conversation in which someone was insincere with you. How did you feel about that interaction? Why is sincerity in relationships so important?

2. Do you think that ultimately, no matter what we believe about God, we will all end up at the same place as long as we are sincere in what we believe? What is the basis for your answer?

3. Have you experienced a situation in which someone you know was sincere but sincerely wrong? Briefly tell about it. What makes that experience so tragic?

4. Suppose that in the realm of religion, the only thing that mattered was sincerity. What would be the benefits of such a system? What might be some disadvantages?

> I have something to say to the religionist who feels atheists never say anything positive: You are an intelligent human being. Your life is valuable for its own sake. You are not second-class in the universe, deriving meaning and purpose from some other mind. You are not inherently evil—you are inherently human, possessing the positive rational potential to help make this a world of morality, peace and joy. Trust yourself.
>
> —Dan Barker,
> *Losing Faith in Faith*

5. Consider the following statement: "One who does a good deed with an evil motive is an evil person, and one who does an evil deed by accident with a good motive is not an evil person." Do you agree? Why or why not?

6. In a conversation on *The Dick Cavett Show* many years ago, the archbishop of Canterbury and Jane Fonda exchanged the following dialogue.

> Archbishop: "Jesus is the Son of God, you know."
>
> Jane Fonda: "Maybe he is for you, but he's not for me."
>
> Archbishop: "Well, either he is or he isn't."

Do you agree or disagree with the archbishop's response? What role does sincerity play in determining the truth behind these statements?

There is a way that seems right to a man, but in the end it leads to death.

—Proverbs 16:25

7. Anatole France once said, "If 50 million people believe a foolish thing, it is still a foolish thing." Would it make any difference if the 50 million people had sincere intentions? Explain.

STRAIGHT TALK

Sincerely Wrong

There are times when sincerity is enough, yet there are other times when it doesn't do much good. In his book *Give Me an Answer,* Cliffe Knechtle tells this story to illustrate that point.

Suppose a student didn't study for an exam. Instead she just went into the test and allowed her inner being to flow out all over her exam paper. Then when she received the result she went to the professor and said, "Professor, how could you flunk me? I really expressed the way I felt on this exam. I was honest. I was sincere."

The professor would look her in the face and say, "You were honestly wrong. You were sincerely mistaken. You flunk."

For some reason, many people understand that it is possible to be sincerely wrong in a wide variety of situations in our world; but when it comes to religion and God, the popular opinion is that sincerity matters more than what might really be right. This is tragic because it leads to complacency and misses the entire purpose of life: to live with God and enjoy him both now and forever.

The "mountain analogy" pictures God at the peak of the mountain with man down at the base. The story of religion is the account of man's effort to move from the base of the mountain to the peak of fellowship and communion with God. The mountain has many roads. Some of the roads go up the mountain by a direct route. Other roads wind in circuitous fashion all over the mountain, but eventually reach the top. Thus, according to the proponents of this analogy, all religious roads, though they differ in route, ultimately arrive at the same place.

—R. C. Sproul,
Reason to Believe

8. Based on the above illustration, someone can be sincerely wrong. Do you believe that this conclusion also applies to one's religion and relationship with God? What exceptions or comparisons can you identify? Explain.

HEART OF THE MATTER

9. Do you find that some people in your world (neighborhood, business, family, etc.) often have an insincere streak but don't always see it in themselves? Explain.

10. What about you? Is it important for you to be sincere in all your dealings? What tempts you to *not* be sincere?

11. Do you have any fears about being sincerely wrong about your spiritual beliefs? Explain.

STRAIGHT TALK

Truth Matters

Sincerity without truth is usually more harmful than helpful. However, sincerity combined with the truth makes all the difference in the world. Consider this example from Cliffe Knechtle in *Give Me an Answer.*

> In medicine, truth is vital. It would be cruel (should we say evil?) if a doctor looked a patient in the face and said, "You have a malignant tumor that is spreading throughout your body. It really doesn't matter though. You can either go home and allow the tumor to continue to consume your body, or else you can allow me to surgically remove it. Either way is fine. Just be a nice guy and everything will turn out all right."
>
> The doctor knows that the tumor is destroying that human life, and motivated by truth he will look into the face of the patient and say, "My friend, there is a tumor that is eating away at your body. It will end in death. But I can surgically remove it to help prolong your life. I would encourage you with everything in me to allow me to do the surgery." That is virtuous — sincerity with truth.

12. To what degree are you interested in sincerely basing your beliefs on the truth? How difficult is that for you to do? Explain.

CHARTING YOUR JOURNEY

13. Check the statement(s) below that best describes your position at this point. Share your selection with the rest of the group and give reasons for your response.

_____ I still think sincerity is enough when it comes to beliefs about God.

_____ It bothers me that God would turn his back on someone who was sincere but wrong.

_____ I think truth is all that matters, even if your motives are off.

_____ There must be some sort of middle ground; how could God *not* care about sincerity?

_____ I am still confused about the issue of sincerity.

_____ It bothers me that some people I know and love may be sincere but wrong in what they believe—and therefore have no chance of "making the grade."

_____ I think a balance of truth and sincerity is what matters.

14. On a scale from one to ten, place an X near the spot and phrase that best describes your position at this point. Share your selection with the rest of the group and give reasons for placing your X where you did.

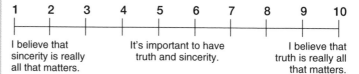

| 1 | 2 | 3 | 4 | 5 | 6 | 7 | 8 | 9 | 10 |

I believe that sincerity is really all that matters.　　　It's important to have truth and sincerity.　　　I believe that truth is really all that matters.

Scripture for Further Study

- 1 Chronicles 28:9
- Isaiah 5:20
- Isaiah 55:8–9
- Matthew 12:33–37
- Matthew 21:28–32
- Luke 10:30–42

- Luke 12:16–21
- Luke 16:19–31
- John 14:6, 15, 21
- Acts 3:22
- Acts 16:22–34
- 1 John 2:3–6

What's So Different About Christianity?

All About the Same

Howard stared at the shelves of spaghetti sauce, smoothing his beard. Rows of options forced him to compare sizes and brands. It was hard to read the small print, and he got confused trying to remember which brand had green peppers and which didn't.

"Doesn't look like they're much different," he concluded aloud as he placed a jar into his cart. An elderly woman carrying a shopping basket and clenching a wad of coupons leaned toward him and whispered, "Yes, there is a difference. It's the price!" She snatched the generic brand and scurried off.

On his way home Howard stopped at the gas station. He hesitated for a moment before pulling up to the pump. Regular, plus, or premium-grade? He remembered his friend telling him that some newer, high-performance engines require high octane, but his five-year-old car certainly wasn't high-performance. It shouldn't matter if he chose the high or regular octane. He drove to the first available pump and quickly began filling up the car with plus-grade gas.

As Howard drove off, the radio blared an advertisement for a new Internet package. Did he already have some of the same features with his current service provider, or would this be a better choice? He jotted down the phone number but then thought, *Why bother? I might as well stick with what I have now—they're all about the same.*

When he finally arrived home, a colleague from work called. "What do you think about the new boss?"

"He doesn't seem much different than our old boss," Howard replied. "They both want the same thing out of us: show up on time, meet deadlines, and complete our work."

After dinner Howard's wife said, "Hey, I was thinking maybe we could visit a church somewhere this Sunday. Where do you think we should go?"

Howard paused for a moment. "Well, they're probably all about the same. Just grab the Yellow Pages and pick one."

With nearly limitless choices on everything from restaurant entrees to automobiles, how can we ever expect to gain enough knowledge to choose the absolute best of anything? In the final analysis, how different are all these choices anyway—and does it really matter? Doesn't it all just boil down to preference—not better or best? Certainly there's no one "right" product everyone should buy.

Is the same true of religion? How can we be expected to understand the subtle nuances of different faiths? Why bother trying, when they all seem about the same? And since they're very similar, does it really matter which one we follow?

> There is no one alive today who knows enough to say with confidence whether one religion has been greater than all others.
>
> —Arnold Toynbee

OPEN FOR DISCUSSION

1. Do you know anyone who is a faithful follower of any of the major world religions other than Christianity (Buddhism, Hinduism,

Islam, or Judaism)? What characterizes someone who practices that particular religion?

2. Give a one- or two-sentence summary of what you know about one of the following major world religions: Hinduism, Buddhism, Islam, or Judaism.

World Religion	Date Started	Founder	Scripture
Hinduism	2000 B.C.	No one founder (developed over many centuries)	Vedas, Upanishads, Bhagavad Gita
Buddhism	525 B.C.	Siddhartha Gautama (the Buddha or Enlightened One)	Tripitaka
Islam	A.D. 622	Muhammad	Koran
Judaism	2000 B.C.	Abraham (and later Moses, the lawgiver)	Torah (the Old Testament part of the Bible)
Christianity	A.D. 30–33	Jesus Christ	Bible

3. To what extent do (and should) the scripture of a religion and the credibility of its founder influence your willingness to accept its teachings? What other factors attract you to— or repel you from—a religion?

STRAIGHT TALK

Basic Teachings and Doctrines

Hinduism: Polytheism — many gods including Vishnu, Shiva, and Brahman (ultimately pantheism — everything is God).

- Reincarnation (samsara): We are all on an endless cycle of birth, death, and rebirth (may come back as animals, vegetables, or insects — not just as humans).
- Law of karma: All present experiences, good and bad, are retribution for how we lived in past lives.
- Yoga: Disciplines to develop to enable one to overcome bad karma and be "yoked" with the One.

Buddhism: No ultimate, personal God — agnosticism (nothing is certain).

- The Four Noble Truths:
    1. Suffering is universal.
    2. The cause of suffering is craving.
    3. The cure for suffering is through working toward the cessation of craving.
    4. The way to cease craving is to follow the Middle Way: the Noble Eightfold Path.

Islam: Allah is the one true God.

- Allah has many prophets; Muhammad is the last and greatest.

- Four inspired books, of which the Koran is superior.
- The Five Pillars of Faith.
- There are many angels, both good and bad.
- There will be a judgment day with a heaven and hell to follow.

Judaism: Worship and pursue a personal God.

- Man is born without sin and makes choices to observe the laws given by God, repents as needed.
- The Messiah is yet to come.

Christianity: Worship and pursue a personal God through Jesus Christ.

- One God, three persons (Father, Son, and Holy Spirit).
- Man is born in sin and needs to be reconciled to God.
- Jesus is the only Son of God.
- Jesus died and rose again from the dead to make payment for sin.
- There will be a judgment day with a heaven and hell to follow.

---

4. Describe some differences you notice in the basic beliefs and teachings among the above five religions. (Include other differences you know of that are not on the chart.) How significant do these differences seem to you?

5. Do you think it is possible that all five of these religions are teaching truth? Why or why not? How do these religions address meaning-of-life issues (life's problems and life's answers)?

STRAIGHT TALK

View of Salvation

Hinduism: The Four Yogas

- The way of knowledge
- The way of devotion
- The way of action
- The way of meditation

Buddhism: The Noble Eightfold Path

- Right viewpoint
- Right aspiration
- Right speech
- Right behavior
- Right occupation
- Right effort
- Right mindfulness
- Right meditation

Islam: Five Pillars of Faith

- The Muslim must publicly repeat the Shahadah (statement of belief): "There is no god but Allah and Muhammad is his prophet."
- Prayers: Five times a day the Muslim must kneel and bow in the direction of the holy city, Mecca — the city where Allah revealed the Koran to Muhammad.

- Alms: The Muslim must give one-fortieth of his income to the poor.
- The Fast of Ramadan: During this month, Muslims must fast during the day.
- Pilgrimage to Mecca: The Hajj must be performed once in a Muslim's lifetime.

Judaism

- Ethnic heritage — the chosen people of God
- Good moral behavior
- Right attitudes
- Repentance (teshuva)

---

6. What do you observe as a common link among all four of these religions, especially concerning how a person obtains salvation?

7. To what extent could a person be confident that he or she has measured up to the required standards of any of these four religions? Explain.

STRAIGHT TALK

The Christian View of Salvation

Christianity

- Jesus Christ paid the price for our sins and provides a free gift of salvation that cannot be earned.
- Confess and repent of sin.
- Believe and receive God's offer of forgiveness through his Son, Jesus Christ.

8. How do the other world religions contrast or compare with the above outline of salvation from the teachings of Christianity?

> It is by grace you have been saved, through faith—and this not from yourselves, it is the gift of God—not by works, so that no one can boast.
>
> —Ephesians 2:8–9

STRAIGHT TALK

Ultimate Destiny

Hinduism: moksha—total liberation and oneness with the All (absorption like a drop in the ocean of the universe)

Buddhism: nirvana—extinction of desire and release from the unending cycle of suffering

Islam: paradise (or if evil, hell)

Judaism: whatever God provides (not clear about heaven or hell)

Christianity: heaven (eternal connection with God) or hell (eternal separation from God)

9. Are you aware of any evidence that shows that reincarnation (the transmigration of souls into new forms after death, based on karma) occurs? Do you think Hinduism or Buddhism would make sense if reincarnation was *not* true? Why or why not?

> It was more than I could believe that Jesus was the only incarnate Son of God. And that only he who believed in him would have everlasting life. If God could have sons, all of us were his sons. If Jesus was like God . . . then all men were like God and could be God himself.
>
> —Mohandas Gandhi

HEART OF THE MATTER

10. Which of the five major religions summarized in this lesson make sense to you? Which makes the most sense? The least?

11. How do you feel about the fact that people believe so differently—and strongly—when it comes to religion? What reasons can you give for these differences?

> Jesus was only a messenger of Allah. . . . Far is it removed from His transcendent majesty that He should have a son.
>
> —Surah 4:171, the Koran

12. On what will you base your decision as to which religion, if any, is right for you?

CHARTING YOUR JOURNEY

13. On a scale from one to ten, place an X near the spot and phrase that best describes you. Share your selection with the rest of the group and give reasons for placing your X where you did.

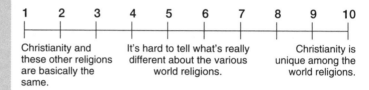

| 1 | 2 | 3 | 4 | 5 | 6 | 7 | 8 | 9 | 10 |

Christianity and these other religions are basically the same.

It's hard to tell what's really different about the various world religions.

Christianity is unique among the world religions.

Scripture for Further Study

- Psalm 118:8
- Ecclesiastes 7:20
- Isaiah 64:6
- Matthew 5:17–20
- Matthew 7:13–14
- Matthew 10:32–33
- John 3:16
- John 8:45–47
- John 14:6
- John 17:17b
- Acts 4:12, 23–30
- Romans 3:10, 21–25

- Romans 6:23
- Romans 10
- 1 Corinthians 1:18–19
- Galatians 3:19–25
- Ephesians 2:8–9
- Colossians 2:9–15
- Hebrews 9:22
- Hebrews 12:2
- Titus 3:5
- 1 John 1:8–9
- 1 John 3:4–5
- 1 John 4:1–3

Aren't Mormons and Jehovah's Witnesses Christians, Too?

Just Another Brand of Christianity?

They've knocked on my door, and I'll bet they've knocked on yours. Members of religious sects, notably the Mormons and Jehovah's Witnesses, are aggressive in their attempts to introduce others to their faith. They're very friendly and polite. They say they believe in Jesus but that their organization best represents him—and that if you want truth, you must follow their teachings.

If you take the time to speak with these folks, they claim to have had life-changing experiences. They say that serving God now motivates the good they do. It is hard to imagine that such religious people who claim to be Christians and believe in God would be turned away by the God they say they obey.

So what's the problem with groups like Mormons and Jehovah's Witnesses? Aren't they both part of the worldwide Christian movement, with just a few minor differences? With so many divisions within Christianity—Baptist, Methodist, Lutheran—isn't it really just nuances that separate various believers in Jesus? Lutherans don't agree with everything Presbyterians do, right? All the different groups have their peculiarities. Then why view Mormons and Jehovah's Witnesses any differently? Why draw the line arbitrarily and say one group is a denomination and is fine, yet another group is a sect to be avoided? Besides, how could an erroneous religion produce such nice people? Didn't Jesus say we would know false prophets by their fruit? Where's the rotten fruit that should accompany a false source—if in fact it is false?

It leaves you wondering: *Why all this fuss? Aren't Mormons and Jehovah's Witnesses Christians, too?*

OPEN FOR DISCUSSION

1. What's your reaction to people who proselytize (try to convert others to their religion)?

2. How would you describe people you know who were raised in (or converted to) the Mormon or Jehovah's Witnesses religions?

3. What do you think Mormons and Jehovah's Witnesses have in common with other Christian believers? What have you discovered to be distinguishing beliefs and/or practices of Mormons and Jehovah's Witnesses?

4. How would you define a cult? Do you think the Mormons or the Jehovah's Witnesses fall into your definition of a cult? Why or why not?

STRAIGHT TALK

Defining a Cult

Outlined below are four simple questions that can be applied to the doctrine of any religion to help determine whether its teachings are mainstream or cultic. If the answers to these questions differ from what the Bible teaches, that religion can be considered to be a sect or cult rather than a Christian denomination. Note: This test has nothing to do with issues such as mind control or other aspects of a religious group's practices. It is merely a test for orthodoxy (biblical conformity).

C — Christ: Who is he? (The Bible: Jesus Christ is the unique Son of God — the God-man.)

U — Ultimate authority: Where does it come from? (The Bible: The Bible alone — no special interpreters are required.)

L — Life eternal: How do we get it? (The Bible: By God's grace through faith alone — it can't be earned.)

T — Teachers: What is their role? (The Bible: To expound on Scripture but not to take the Holy Spirit's place or be a final interpreter.)

> Be it known that no other system of theology even claims, or has ever attempted to harmonize in itself every statement of the Bible, yet nothing short of this can we claim.
>
> —Charles Taze Russell, Jehovah's Witnesses, *Studies in the Scriptures, 1:348*

5. Do you agree or disagree with these diagnostic questions to identify a cult? Explain.

STRAIGHT TALK

Basic Facts About Mormons and Jehovah's Witnesses

Religion	Date Started	Founder	Scripture
Mormonism (The Church of Jesus Christ of Latter-day Saints)	1830	Joseph Smith Jr.	the Bible, plus the Book of Mormon, Doctrine and Covenants, Pearl of Great Price
Jehovah's Witnesses (Watchtower Bible and Tract Society)	1874	Charles Taze Russell	the Bible (prefer New World Translation of Holy Scriptures)

STRAIGHT TALK

Basic Teachings and Doctrines

Mormonism

The Book of Mormon is considered to be the Word of God for our times (more accurate than the Bible).

God is a human being who became a god.

Christ is also a human being who became a god.

Any Mormon may attain godhood — there are many gods.

Males must practice polygamy in the afterlife to reach the highest level of heaven.

Salvation by faith, plus works, plus baptism.

Baptism for the dead procures eternal life for them.

Jehovah's Witnesses

One God, no Trinity.

Jesus Christ is not God in human flesh but a created being (Michael the Archangel in human form).

Salvation is based on works (obedience, baptism, continued learning, recruiting others).

144,000 witnesses will be chosen by God to be special leaders in heaven (the rest — the vast majority — will live on a renewed earth).

Bodily resurrection of Christ denied — spiritual only.

Christ "returned" in 1914 and now rules from heaven.

No hell, only annihilation of the wicked.

Christianity

The Bible is considered the inerrant Word of God.

God in three persons (Father, Son, and Holy Spirit).

Christ is God's Son (completely human and completely God).

Salvation by faith, not by works.

Baptism symbolizes salvation.

6. Review the information in the previous two Straight Talks about the Mormons and the Jehovah's Witnesses. What makes their teachings and doctrines very different from the Bible's teachings?

My object in going to inquire of the Lord was to know which of all the sects was right. . . . I was answered that I must join none of them, for they were all wrong and [God] said that all their creeds were an abomination in His sight; that those professors were all corrupt; that "they draw near to me with their lips, but their hearts are far from me. . . ." He again forbade me to join with any of them.

—Joseph Smith, Mormon founder

7. What facts most intrigue you about the above two religions? What is appealing— or unappealing—to you about Mormonism and Jehovah's Witnesses?

8. In your opinion, are the differences between the Mormon and the Jehovah's Witnesses religions and Christianity significant enough for these two religions to warrant the label "cult"? Why or why not?

9. What, in your view, explains how a group can misstate biblical truths and teach such different doctrines, yet produce people who in most respects seem "Christian" in their behavior?

10. What "fruit" besides living a good life could Jesus have been referring to when he distinguished between true and false teachers (or prophets) by saying, "By their fruit you will recognize them" (Matthew 7:15–23)?

11. How does it make you feel when you hear Christians say that the Mormons and the Jehovah's Witnesses are cults or sects? Is this spiritual bigotry? Explain your answer.

> I told you that you would die in your sins; if you do not believe that I am the one I claim to be, you will indeed die in your sins.
>
> —Jesus (John 8:24)

12. How do you explain why the Mormons and the Jehovah's Witnesses are growing in such large numbers? If a group is not in harmony with the Bible's teachings, why do you think God would let it have increasing influence?

STRAIGHT TALK

Warnings from the Bible

There were also false prophets among the people, just as there will be false teachers among you. They will secretly introduce destructive heresies, even denying the sovereign Lord who bought them—bringing swift destruction on themselves.

—2 Peter 2:1

Watch out for false prophets. They come to you in sheep's clothing, but inwardly they are ferocious wolves.

—Matthew 7:15

Such men are false apostles, deceitful workmen, masquerading as apostles of Christ.

—2 Corinthians 11:13

Ongoing, healthy questioning of one's own beliefs is a good thing. It is crucial to carefully examine the teachings behind Christianity in order to gain confidence and assurance that Christianity is truly from God. By continually testing the claims of any church or leader (including our own) against the Bible, we can have reasonable certainty of what we believe. There is no room for smug or glib confidence about spiritual matters; our lives must be based on a continuing examination and re-examination of truth.

13. If sincere members of groups like these can be mistaken in their fundamental beliefs, what assurance do you have that you are correct about *your* beliefs? Can anyone really know for sure that he or she is right? Explain your answer.

CHARTING YOUR JOURNEY

14. On a scale from one to ten, place an X near the spot and phrase that best describes you. Share your selection with the rest of the group and give reasons for placing your X where you did.

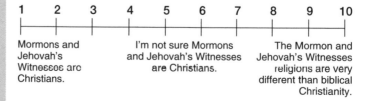

Scripture for Further Study

- Deuteronomy 13:1–5
- Psalm 118:8
- Proverbs 30:5–6
- Isaiah 64:6
- Matthew 7:15–20
- Mark 9:7
- John 1:1–18
- John 10
- John 14:7–10
- John 20:28
- Romans 9:5

- 1 Corinthians 1:18–19
- 1 Corinthians 2:14
- Galatians 2:15–21
- Ephesians 2:8–9
- Philippians 2:5–11
- Colossians 1:15–20
- Titus 2:13; 3:5
- Hebrews 1:2
- 1 John 4:1–3
- Revelation 22:18–19

Is Jesus Really the Only Way to God?

Members Only?

Have you ever tried to join a "members only" organization, only to be refused because you didn't fit the profile? Anyone who's ever known that kind of rejection would describe it as one of the worst feelings imaginable. Yet thousands of clubs and organizations function with such requirements. Looking from the outside in, you may view those inside as condescending snobs. They seem to have no feelings about those left outside. Is their world really so small that nobody matters except their elite few?

There's another group who seem equally exclusive, if not more so. But the stakes are much higher than being denied access to certain facilities or privileges. In this case it is a matter of life and death—and eternity. These "condescending snobs" say that Jesus is the only way to God and leave everyone else outside God's kingdom.

The only way? How can it be that there is only one way to God, to salvation, to eternal life? That's the same kind of condescension for which the religious leaders in Jesus' time were famous. They had set up a religious system with themselves at the center. Jesus reserved his harshest words for these religious leaders—he called them snakes!

Surely Jesus, who represents love and acceptance, wouldn't insist that there is only one way to God. Surely the generosity and unconditional love Jesus talked about will give us a break even if we've not chosen to accept him as the only way. Isn't it enough if we just mind our own business and go about living day to day without opposing God? Doesn't God understand our hearts, even if our outward actions don't always conform to a perfect standard?

"Members Only" sure doesn't sound like the kind of kingdom most of us want to be a part of. Certainly, the God who made billions of people must enjoy them—including all their differences. Doesn't he want everyone to be in the same big gathering up in heaven, regardless of socioeconomic, personal, or even spiritual status?

Why would God be a snob?

OPEN FOR DISCUSSION

1. What is your immediate reaction to the claim that Jesus Christ is the only way to God? How do you suppose most people react to this claim?

2. What are some objections that come to mind concerning the claim that Jesus is the only way? Describe a path of salvation that is *not* exclusive and that would make more sense to those troubled by the "one way" proposal.

3. Do you think the Bible specifically teaches that Jesus is the only way to God? Why? Cite a couple examples to support your answer, if possible.

4. Select *one* of the Bible passages from the list below and put it into your own words.

> [Jesus said,] "I am the way and the truth and the life. No one comes to the Father except through me."
>
> —John 14:6

> Salvation is found in no one else, for there is no other name under heaven given to men by which we must be saved.
>
> —Acts 4:12

> Whoever believes in him is not condemned, but whoever does not believe stands condemned already because he has not believed in the name of God's one and only Son.
>
> —John 3:18

[Jesus said,] "I told you that you would die in your sins; if you do not believe that I am the one I claim to be, you will indeed die in your sins."

—John 8:24

This is the testimony: God has given us eternal life, and this life is in his Son. He who has the Son has life; he who does not have the Son of God does not have life. I write these things to you who believe in the name of the Son of God so that you may know that you have eternal life.

—1 John 5:11–13

5. Based on the above list of Scripture passages, explain your reaction to the following statement: "Christianity does not claim that Jesus is the only way to God."

6. Assuming Christianity does indeed assert that Jesus is the only way, what reasons might people give for viewing this claim as false?

STRAIGHT TALK

Three Common Objections

There are three common objections to the assertion that Jesus Christ is the only way to God.

A. About 75 percent of the world population is not Christian — how could so many people all be wrong? Far too many people do not believe in Christianity; therefore, it cannot be the only way.

B. Really nice people with good intentions do not believe in Jesus. Sincere people ought to be accepted by God on the basis of their strong convictions; therefore, Christianity cannot be the only way.

C. Christianity's claims are exclusive and narrow. Any system that's narrow-minded, limited, and bigoted is false; therefore, it cannot be the only way.

7. Each of the above objections is based on unspoken assumptions about how one determines what is true. Match each objection listed above with its corresponding assumption listed below. Explain your answer.

_____ Intensity of belief ensures truth.
_____ Anything intolerant negates truth.
_____ Popular opinion defines truth.

STRAIGHT TALK

Three Assumptions Examined

Below are three assumptions commonly made about truth, each followed by a statement that directly contradicts the assumption (Ken Boa and Larry Moody, *I'm Glad You Asked*).

A. *Popular opinion defines truth.* For centuries popular opinion stated that the earth was flat. Today the scientific consensus is that the earth is spherical.

B. *Intensity of belief ensures truth.* Some years ago Jim Marshall of the Minnesota Vikings picked up a fumble and fought off tacklers repeatedly until he crossed the goal line. Marshall, however, crossed the wrong goal line and scored for the wrong team.

C. *Anything intolerant negates truth.* The fact that one plus one will always equal two is very narrow, but it is also right. Landing an airplane requires some very narrow and restricted specifications. Engines that run on only unleaded fuel are very exclusive.

Suppose our community passed a unanimous resolution to suspend the law of gravity an hour a day, from 8:00 to 9:00 A.M. Who would join me in jumping off the roof to try it out? Suppose we passed the resolution three times? I still wouldn't get any takers. We do not determine socially the penalty for violating the law of gravity; the penalty is inherent in the violation. Even if we passed motions till the cows came home, the fact would remain that if you jumped off the roof someone would have to pick you up with a shovel!

—Paul Little, *How to Give Away Your Faith*

8. Do you think the above assumptions are still true in light of the contradicting observations? How does your answer apply to similar truths in the spiritual realm?

STRAIGHT TALK

Four Possible Conclusions

In his book *How to Give Away Your Faith* Paul Little states the following challenge.

> Since you don't believe Jesus Christ was the Truth, which of the other three possibilities about Jesus Christ do you believe? There are only four possible conclusions about Jesus Christ and his claims. He was either a liar, a lunatic, a legend or the Truth. The person who doesn't believe he was the Truth must label him as a liar, a lunatic, or a legend.

9. If Jesus was not who he claimed to be (the only way to God), which of the other alternatives listed above seems most reasonable to you? Why?

HEART OF THE MATTER

10. How does concluding that there is more than one way to God make a mockery out of Christ's death?

> In light of mankind's universal rebellion against God, the issue is not why is there only one way, but why is there any way at all?
>
> —R. C. Sproul,
> *Reason to Believe*

11. If Jesus Christ really is the only way to God, what impact would wholeheartedly believing this have on our lives and relationships?

CHARTING YOUR JOURNEY

12. On a scale from one to ten, place an X near the spot and phrase that best describes you. Share your selection with the rest of the group and give reasons for placing your X where you did.

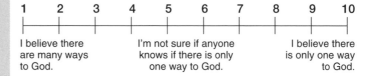

1   2   3   4   5   6   7   8   9   10

I believe there are many ways to God.

I'm not sure if anyone knows if there is only one way to God.

I believe there is only one way to God.

Scripture for Further Study

- Isaiah 55:8–9
- Proverbs 14:12
- Proverbs 30:5–6
- Matthew 7:13–27
- Matthew 10:32–33
- Matthew 24:35
- Mark 1:15
- Luke 9:57–62
- John 10:33–38
- John 14:6
- John 17:17b
- Romans 1–3
- Romans 5:12–21
- Romans 11:33–36
- Hebrews 1
- 1 Peter 1:24–25

What Happens to People Who've Never Heard of Jesus?

That Sinking Feeling

The alarm went off, but Sam was already up and studying for the big final. This had been one of the toughest college courses he had ever taken. He went to every class, took copious notes, and had even organized a study group. He had spent hours outlining and studying every chapter in the giant textbook. He had—with the permission of his professor—gotten hold of old tests and quizzes and poured over them. He knew the material inside and out. He was ready, and this was the day he would prove it.

He was the first one to the classroom. He found a seat close to the front of the room. When everyone had arrived and the professor had handed out the exam, Sam took a deep, confident breath and opened up his booklet.

But something was terribly wrong. The first question didn't make any sense to him. The second question was just as confusing . . . and the third. He started to panic. He continued to flip through the booklet. He didn't know any of these answers! The questions seemed to be about topics never covered in class or even mentioned in his textbook. What was going on? He grabbed his test and raced to the professor's desk.

"Excuse me, sir," he started, "why are we being tested on material we've never heard of?"

The professor only shrugged. "This is important information," he stated, pointing to his watch, "and you've got only forty-eight minutes left."

"I'm sure it is important—but you never covered it or told us our grade would be based on it!" pleaded Sam.

"I'm the professor, not you! Do you dare question my judgment when I have the power of your grade in my hands?"

Sam shook his head in disbelief and shuffled back to his desk.

How unfair! Why would a professor hold a class responsible for material never covered? What kind of person would wield power so unfairly?

In the same way, does God hold people responsible for information they've never had the opportunity to hear? If the message of Christ is so critical, why doesn't a loving God make it so loud and clear that no one will miss it? And what about religious, God-believing people outside Christian influence? Is the "crime" of not hearing about Jesus worthy of hell? It just doesn't seem right that people could be excluded from heaven on the basis of circumstances beyond their control. What about babies who die, the mentally disabled, lost tribes in jungles who know nothing of the outside world? Will they all flunk the ultimate test just because they've never heard the truth? What kind of God would set up this kind of system? Not a very fair one.

Yet if the claims of Christianity are true, that's exactly what it appears he's done!

God has infinite wisdom, goodness, and power. . . . Now, my friend, can prophecies or miracles convince you or me that infinite benevolence, wisdom, and power, created, and preserves for a time innumerable millions, to make them miserable forever, for his own glory? Wretch! Is he vain, tickled with adulation, exulting and triumphing in his power and the sweetness of his vengeance? Pardon me, my Maker, for these awful questions. My answer to them is always ready. I believe no such things. My adoration of the author of the universe is too profound and too sincere.

—John Adams, in a letter to Thomas Jefferson

1. Do you agree with the saying "Ignorance is bliss"? Why or why not?

I shall only add, respecting myself, that, having experienced the goodness of that Being in conducting me prosperously through a long life, I have no doubt of its continuance in the next, without the smallest conceit of meriting it.

—Benjamin Franklin, shortly before his death

2. What do you think God's opinion is of those who are ignorant of him? Do you think he holds people morally responsible for what they don't know about him?

3. Suppose everyone who has not heard about Jesus Christ is considered spiritually and morally innocent. Why should missionaries be sent all over the world to expose innocent people to a knowledge that could put them at risk of hell (if they reject it)?

Go and make disciples of all nations, baptizing them in the name of the Father and of the Son and of the Holy Spirit.

—Jesus (Matthew 28:19)

STRAIGHT TALK

Innocent or Not?

Are there actually innocent people in our world? The Bible states that every one of us has sinned and fallen short of God's standard (Romans 3:23). In his book *Reason to Believe* R. C. Sproul remarks,

> When we ask, "What happens to the innocent person who has never heard?" we are loading the question with significant assumptions. . . . The innocent person doesn't need to hear of Christ. He has no need of redemption. God never punishes innocent people. The innocent person needs no Savior; he can save himself by his innocence.

Righteousness and justice are the foundation of your throne; love and faithfulness go before you.

—Psalm 89:14

4. Do you agree with the above reasoning? Why or why not?

5. If God is completely righteous and fair in all of his judgments, do you think he will condemn people simply because they never heard the gospel? Explain.

STRAIGHT TALK

Held Accountable

R. C. Sproul *(Reason to Believe)* draws this conclusion: "If God were to punish a person for not responding to a message he had no possibility of hearing, that would be gross injustice; it would be radically inconsistent with God's own revealed justice. We can rest assured that no one is ever punished for rejecting Christ if they've never heard of him. Before we sigh too deep a breath of relief, let us keep in mind that the native is still not off the hook . . . It is precisely at this point that the New Testament locates the universal guilt of man . . . God's wrath is revealed not against innocence or ignorance but against ungodliness and wickedness."

The Bible teaches that all people have a responsibility to acknowledge God as God and admit needing him.

> The wrath of God is being revealed from heaven against all the godlessness and wickedness of men who suppress the truth by their wickedness, since what may be known about God is plain to them, because God has made it plain to them. For since the creation of the world God's invisible qualities — his eternal power and divine nature — have been clearly seen, being understood from what has been made, so that men are without excuse.
>
> — Romans 1:18–20

> All who sin apart from the law will also perish apart from the law, and all who sin under the law will be judged by the law.
>
> — Romans 2:12

> God did not send his Son into the world to condemn the world, but to save the world through him. Whoever believes in him is not condemned, but whoever does not believe stands condemned already because he has not believed in the name of God's one and only Son.
>
> —John 3:17–18

6. What do the above verses say about the amount of spiritual knowledge all people have, regardless of their spiritual heritage? What determines someone's eternal destiny, according to these passages?

7. According to the above verses, what is the basis upon which God finds fault with people? Do you believe that is enough of a basis for condemnation? Why or why not?

STRAIGHT TALK

Those Who've Never Heard

No one knows exactly how to answer the perplexing question "What happens to those who've never heard about Jesus?" But there are some biblical principles that can shed some light on this issue.

- God is righteous and just in all he does — in the end we will all affirm the rightness of his judgments (Psalm 116:5).
- People are not condemned for rejecting a message they never heard — lack of knowledge of Jesus is not the reason people end up in hell (Ephesians 2:1–2).
- People are responsible for the light they have received — and at a minimum everyone has knowledge of God gained through creation and conscience (Psalm 19:1–4; Romans 1:20).
- No one will be in heaven merely because he or she has been sincere and lived a good life — for no one has (Ephesians 2:8–9; Titus 3:5).
- The only reason why people will be in heaven is because of grace personally received, and the only basis for forgiveness clearly outlined in the Bible is Jesus Christ paying the price for each one's sin through his death on the cross (John 1:12; Acts 4:12; Romans 3:22–24; 5:6–8).

8. With the above principles in mind, what conclusions can you draw so far about the destiny of those who have not heard the message of Jesus Christ? Explain.

> He is the Rock, his works are perfect, and all his ways are just. A faithful God who does no wrong, upright and just is he.
>
> —Deuteronomy 32:4

HEART OF THE MATTER

9. What other issues might be at the heart of someone's objection concerning the fate of those who've never heard of Christ?

STRAIGHT TALK

A Response Required

Without a doubt, we can say that all who hear about Jesus Christ have a duty to respond to that message. The message of Jesus doesn't make spiritually healthy people sick, but it offers the possibility of a cure to all who are spiritually ailing (John 5:24). Those who refuse the cure will die of the disease; that much is sure.

10. Do you agree with the above Straight Talk? Why or why not?

11. What is the ultimate relevancy to you personally concerning the question "What will happen to those who never hear about Jesus?"

12. If you believed that Jesus Christ is the only way to God, what responsibility would you feel to inform others about Jesus?

CHARTING YOUR JOURNEY

13. Check the statement(s) below that best describes your position at this point. Share your selection with the rest of the group and give reasons for your response.

_____ Everyone, regardless of their relationship to Christ, will be with God in heaven.

_____ Some people who never heard of Christ will be in heaven, but others won't.

_____ Some people who reject Christ won't be in heaven, but those who never heard of him will be okay.

_____ People who've never heard of Christ will get a second chance after they die.

_____ Everyone will get a second chance after they die.

_____ God makes sure every sincere seeker finds Christ.

_____ Only people who've accepted Christ will be in heaven.

Scripture for Further Study

- Isaiah 55:6–7
- Jonah
- Matthew 10
- Matthew 25:31–46
- Matthew 28:16–20
- Luke 10:1–24

- Acts 1:8
- Acts 17:11
- Romans 1:18–32
- Romans 2:12–16
- Romans 10

Recommended Resources

Ken Boa and Larry Moody, *I'm Glad You Asked* (Chariot Victor, 1995).

Gregory Boyd and Edward Boyd, *Letters from a Skeptic* (Chariot Victor, 1994).

David Hewetson and David Miller. *Christianity Made Simple* (InterVarsity, 1983).

Cliffe Knechtle, *Give Me an Answer* (InterVarsity, 1986).

Cliffe Knechtle, *Help Me Believe* (InterVarsity, 2000).

Peter Kreeft and Ronald Tacelli, *Handbook of Christian Apologetics* (InterVarsity, 1994).

C. S. Lewis, *Mere Christianity* (HarperSanFransisco, 2001).

Paul Little, *Know What You Believe* (Chariot Victor, 1987).

Paul Little, *Know Why You Believe* (InterVarsity, 2000).

Walter Martin, *Kingdom of the Cults* (Bethany, 1997).

Fritz Ridenour, *So What's the Difference?* (Regal, 2001).

Lee Strobel, *The Case for Christ* (Zondervan, 1998).

Lee Strobel, *The Case for Faith* (Zondervan, 2000).

WILLOW
Willow Creek Association

Willow Creek Association
Vision, Training, Resources for Prevailing Churches

This resource was created to serve you and to help you build a local church that prevails. It is just one of many ministry tools that are part of the Willow Creek Resources® line, published by the Willow Creek Association together with Zondervan.

The Willow Creek Association (WCA) was created in 1992 to serve a rapidly growing number of churches from across the denominational spectrum that are committed to helping unchurched people become fully devoted followers of Christ. Membership in the WCA now numbers over 10,000 Member Churches worldwide from more than ninety denominations.

The Willow Creek Association links like-minded Christian leaders with each other and with strategic vision, training, and resources in order to help them build prevailing churches designed to reach their redemptive potential. Here are some of the ways the WCA does that.

- **Prevailing Church Conference**—an annual two-and-a-half day event, held at Willow Creek Community Church in South Barrington, Illinois, to help pioneering church leaders raise up a volunteer core while discovering new and innovative ways to build prevailing churches that reach unchurched people.

- **Leadership Summit**—a once-a-year, two-and-a-half-day conference to envision and equip Christians with leadership gifts and responsibilities. Presented live at Willow Creek as well as via satellite broadcast to over sixty locations across North America, this event is designed to increase the leadership effectiveness of pastors, ministry staff, volunteer church leaders, and Christians in the marketplace.

- **Ministry-Specific Conferences**—throughout each year the WCA hosts a variety of conferences and training events—both at Willow Creek's main campus and off-site, across the U.S. and around the world—targeting church leaders in ministry-specific areas such as: evangelism, the arts, children, students, small groups, preaching and teaching, spiritual formation, spiritual gifts, raising up resources, etc.

- **Willow Creek Resources®**—to provide churches with trusted and field-tested ministry resources in such areas as leadership, evangelism, spiritual formation, spiritual gifts, small groups, stewardship, student ministry, children's ministry, the use of the arts—drama, media, contemporary music—and more. For additional information about Willow Creek Resources® call the Customer Service Center at 800-570-9812. Outside the U.S. call 847-765-0070.

- *WillowNet*—the WCA's Internet resource service, which provides access to hundreds of transcripts of Willow Creek messages, drama scripts, songs, videos, and multimedia tools. The system allows users to sort through these elements and download them for a fee. Visit us online at www.willowcreek.com.

- *WCA News*—a quarterly publication to inform you of the latest trends, resources, and information on WCA events from around the world.

- *Defining Moments*—a monthly audio journal for church leaders featuring Bill Hybels and other Christian leaders discussing probing issues to help you discover biblical principles and transferable strategies to maximize your church's redemptive potential.

- *The Exchange*—our online classified ads service to assist churches in recruiting key staff for ministry positions.

- **Member Benefits**—includes substantial discounts to WCA training events, a 20 percent discount on all Willow Creek Resources®, access to a Members-Only section on WillowNet, monthly communications, and more. Member Churches also receive special discounts and premier services through WCA's growing number of ministry partners—Select Service Providers.

For specific information about WCA membership, upcoming conferences, and other ministry services contact:

Willow Creek Association
P.O. Box 3188, Barrington, IL 60011-3188
Phone: 847-570-9812
Fax: 847-765-5046
www.willowcreek.com

TOUGH QUESTIONS

Garry Poole and Judson Poling

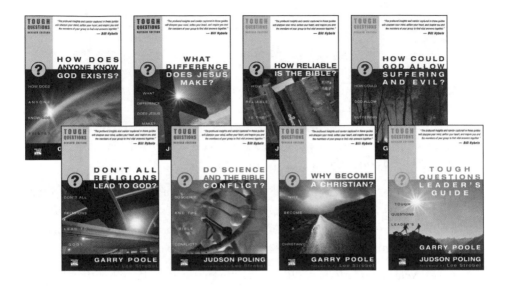

"The profound insights and candor captured in these guides will sharpen your mind, soften your heart, and inspire you and the members of your group to find vital answers together."   —Bill Hybels

This second edition of Tough Questions, designed for use in any small group setting, is ideal for use in seeker small groups. Based on more than five years of field-tested feedback, extensive revisions make this best-selling series easier to use and more appealing than ever for both participants and group leaders.

Softcover

How Does Anyone Know God Exists?	ISBN 0-310-24502-8
What Difference Does Jesus Make?	ISBN 0-310-24503-6
How Reliable Is the Bible?	ISBN 0-310-24504-4
How Could God Allow Suffering and Evil?	ISBN 0-310-24505-2
Don't All Religions Lead to God?	ISBN 0-310-24506-0
Do Science and the Bible Conflict?	ISBN 0-310-24507-9
Why Become a Christian?	ISBN 0-310-24508-7
Leader's Guide	ISBN 0-310-24509-5

Pick up a copy at your favorite local bookstore today!

WILLOW CREEK
RESOURCES

ZONDERVAN™

GRAND RAPIDS, MICHIGAN 49530 USA
WWW.ZONDERVAN.COM

THE THREE HABITS OF HIGHLY CONTAGIOUS CHRISTIANS

Garry Poole

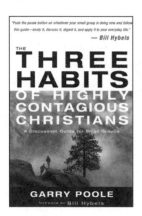

A small group discussion guide that will ignite the heart to reach seekers for Christ.

Living an intentionally contagious Christian life really matters! It's worth the effort and risks involved. *The Three Habits of Highly Contagious Christians* will help you reach out to seekers naturally by

1. building relationships
2. sharing a verbal witness
3. inviting people to outreach events

Discover how to cultivate authentic relationships with seekers, not as projects to work on but as friends and companions with common interests. You'll learn practical ways to build bridges of trust while checking yourself for the underlying attitudes that drive seekers away. From being on the lookout for windows of opportunity to talk with seekers about Christ, to bringing them to a church service or outreach, this study helps you find ways to bring people to Christ easily and naturally.

Each session begins with a thought-provoking story, then uses questions that generate honest, open group discussion. Exercises encourage participants to apply principles to their own lives. *The Three Habits of Highly Contagious Christians* challenges believers to individually commit to specific choices that could make all the difference in the lives of seeking friends and family members.

Softcover: ISBN 0-310-24496-X

Pick up a copy at your favorite local bookstore today!

GRAND RAPIDS, MICHIGAN 49530 USA

WWW.ZONDERVAN.COM